Explore
Music
through
History

David Wheway and
Shelagh Thomson

16 varied national curriculum
Music activities linked to the
History attainment targets

Music Department
OXFORD UNIVERSITY PRESS
Oxford and New York

Oxford University Press, Walton Street, Oxford OX2 6DP, England

Oxford is a trade mark of Oxford University Press

© David Wheway and Shelagh Thomson, 1993

With the exception of the line drawings which may be reproduced for non-commercial use within the classroom, no part of this publication may be reproduced, stored in a retrieval system, or transmitted in any form or by any means, electronic, mechanical, photocopying, recording, or otherwise, without the prior permission of the Publishers.

First published 1993
ISBN 0 19 321871 2
Design and illustration by Creative Intelligence, Bristol
Printed in Great Britain by Caligraving Ltd., Thetford, Norfolk

Contents

4 **Introduction**
  List of Activities
8 Transport Through the Ages
10 Robin Hood Meets Little John
11 Lifeline
12 Greek Mythology
14 The Olympics
16 Ancient Egypt
17 Roman Britain
18 Tudor and Stuart Composers
19 The Gunpowder Plot
20 Civil War
22 The Plague
24 The Great Fire of London
25 Victorian Children
26 Victorian Market
28 Modern Influences
30 Timeline
  Appendix
31 Glossary
32 Pentatonic Scales

There are nine books in this series:
Explore Music through
  Art, Geography, History, Maths, Movement,
  Poetry and Rhyme, Science, Stories, Word Games.

SUPPLIED BY:
ARGENT'S (Printed Music)
20 DENMARK STREET
LONDON WC2H 8NE
071-379 3384

Introduction

These booklets are designed for primary teachers who value the role of music in an integrated approach to the curriculum. They are of equal value to those who have little or no experience of teaching music, or those who have responsibility as a music co-ordinator.

By closely relating musical activities to other areas of the curriculum, it is hoped that primary teachers will feel more confident when engaging in musical activities with children.

Within each of the nine booklets in the series, activities are ordered progressively from 'early years' through to upper Key Stage 2.

The appropriateness of any activity will depend on the previous experience of the child or group. For this reason we have not recommended any activity for a specific age group, but have indicated a target Key Stage.

Many activities, especially those primarily concerned with composition, are often best delivered over a number of sessions. This allows time for exploratory work, and also for evaluation, discussion, and development.

Building a Repertoire of Sounds

Children need an ever-increasing knowledge of sounds, and teachers need to be aware of the importance of sound exploration for future musical activities. This repertoire of sounds is especially important when children wish to represent feelings, objects, and other sounds in their compositions.

Body and Vocal Sounds

Children should explore the possibility for sounds made both vocally and with the body. For instance, how many sounds can be made with the throat? ('Ooooh', 'Ahhhh', a hiccup, a cough, a gargle, humming, sighing, panting, etc.) What different sounds can be made by patting different parts of the body? (Cheeks, chest, stomach, thighs, knees, etc.)

Classroom Percussion

Children should be encouraged to find as many different ways as possible to play percussion. Can it be scraped, tapped, shaken, scratched, blown, etc.? When a new sound is found, think about what moods or images it conjures up. Such exploration works well in small groups, using a limited number of instruments. Allow the children time to play new sounds to the rest of the class.

Percussion Resources

Some considerations when building resources:

Do your percussion resources offer a wide choice for creating a variety of sounds?

Are the instruments made from a variety of materials (e.g. wood, metal, plastic, etc.)?

Does the collection contain instruments from different ethnic origins?

Are the instruments of good quality? Remember, as in other areas of the curriculum, poor quality materials (e.g. worn or broken) may lead to poor or disappointing results.

Other Sound Makers

A wide variety of sounds can be made with everyday objects such as paper, kitchen utensils, beads and pulses (e.g. paper tearing, scrunching, flapping; pulses poured into a bucket, swirled around, shaken; pots and pans drum-kit).

When performing any activity, try different combinations of sound, as this adds to the children's exploratory work and their understanding of timbre and texture.

Recording

It is very important that children develop ways of recording their compositions. A variety of ways are suggested throughout the booklets, for example, pictures, symbols, words, letters, and so on. Ensure paper and appropriate recording materials are always available.

Audio as well as video recorders are also valuable resources for recording children's work and development.

The Activities

Suggested Materials

These materials should be useful as a guide for preparing the lessons. They are only suggestions and teachers may wish to select their own materials.

Suggested Listening

Generally, it is a good idea to keep extracts short, e.g. 30–60 seconds in duration. If possible, tape-record extracts beforehand to avoid searching in the lesson.

Most of the suggestions given are easily available in record libraries or through record shops. Many can be found on compilations. Where this is not the case, a reference is given.

The recordings we have recommended should not be considered either obligatory or comprehensive.

Personal collections of recorded music are a valuable resource. However, do avoid limiting the children's listening opportunities to any one type of music.

Attainment Target Boxes

The left-hand box gives an indication of the main focus of each activity, relating to the national curriculum for Music. However, it should be noted that the activities will also offer a variety of other musical experiences.

The right-hand box indicates how the activity may complement work undertaken in another area of the curriculum.

Classroom Organization

For many whole-class activities, a circle of children on a carpet or chairs is ideal. This helps concentration and promotes a feeling of involvement, as well as being practical when it comes to observing other children, whole-group involvement, and passing games. It might be advisable at times to split the class or set into groups.

There are some activities that require little or no percussion, and if you are just starting out you may feel more confident attempting these activities initially.

Handing Out Instruments

Avoid the children making a headlong rush to the music trolley at all costs! Allow the children to collect, or hand out, a few instruments at a time.

- Have the required instruments placed out ready beforehand.
- While listening to instructions, children should place their instruments on the floor in front of them.
- Give out beaters for instruments last.

- Before commencing agree on clear signals for stopping and putting instruments down (e.g. a hand in the air, a finger to the lips, a wink of the eye, etc.).
- Demand an immediate response to these signals.
- Encourage children to treat instruments with respect at all times. (This is not easy if instruments are worn or broken.)

Evaluation and Appraisal

When children are working on a composition, there should be regular evaluation by the teacher, and/or by the children, of how the work is progressing. This will include a great deal of purposeful listening and appraising. The process will in turn help the children in appraising the music of others.

Key Questions for Performers and Audience

Can you tell us about your music?

How did the piece start/finish?

What did you like about it?

What contrasts/changes did the piece contain?

Does the piece fulfil the task set?

Was it performed fluently and appropriately?

Could it have been improved, and if so, how?

Could the piece be extended, and if so, how? (e.g. repetition, contrasts, new material, different instruments, etc.)

Did the audience listen well?

Transport Through the Ages

Suggested Materials
See opposite.

Can the children find sounds to represent the different forms of transport shown here? The various sounds could be put together in order from past to present, or vice versa. The sounds for walking could be used between the other sounds as a repeating pattern.

Extension Activity
The children might like to go on to find symbols to represent the various forms of transport, e.g. footprints for walking, horse shoes for horses, a horn for an early car, puffs of smoke for a steam train, and appropriate logos for modern transport.

Footsteps - tap knees or feet. Claves.

Coconut shells. Vocal 'clip-clop'.
Tapping on woodblock.

Music Attainment Target: 1
Main Focus: Composing
Key Stage: 1

History Attainment Target: 1
Main Focus: Transport

More of previous horse sounds, and
play faster. Vocal post-horn sound.

Vocal chuffing sounds.
Castanets rattling.

Castanets rattling faster than before. Vocal 'brrr',
and horn. Occasional bang on drum.

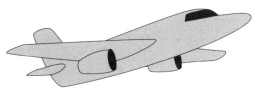

'Vrooom' sounds quickly crescendo (get louder),
and decrescendo (get quieter).

Robin Hood Meets Little John

Suggested Materials

A variety of tuned and untuned percussion. Body and vocal sounds.

This story about Robin Hood, like many myths and legends, offers the opportunity for early composition through sound exploration.

One day Robin Hood was about to cross a bridge above a stream when he noticed a giant of a man about to cross from the other side. Robin Hood shouted to the man to stand aside and let him cross, as there was only room for one person to cross at a time.	Stream - ripple effect on glockenspiels (glissandos up and down), also crumpled paper. Vocal bird sounds. Rubbing paper for leaves of nearby trees. These sounds should play throughout.
The huge man, however, refused to move, and shouted back that Robin Hood should stand aside instead. Robin Hood refused, and the two men began to cross together.	Light and heavy footsteps on claves and drums to represent the two men.
When the two men met in the middle, neither would stand aside, so they began to try to knock each other off the bridge, using their long sticks.	Claves or shinty sticks tapping together.
Eventually both men fell headlong into the water. When they surfaced they looked at each other, and began to roar with laughter. This is how Robin Hood met Little John.	Cymbal crash for the men falling in the water. Fast glissandos on tuned percussion. Vocal 'Splosh'. Vocal laughter, fading along with other sounds.

Having explored the possibilities in each part of the story, order the sounds, and perform them with the story.

Music Attainment Target: 1
Main Focus: Composing
Key Stage: 1

History Attainment Target: 2
Main Focus: Myths and Legends

Lifeline

Suggested Materials

Body and vocal sounds. Access to a variety of percussion.

1. The children make a list of seven or eight memories, starting recently and going back in time.
2. The children find sounds to represent these episodes (see cards below).
3. Once they have sounds for each episode, they play them in order, moving either forward in time, or back, e.g.

---

a) A recent holiday (aged 7).
- vocal seagull sounds
- ripples on xylophone
- patting knees for sandcastles

b) Falling off my bike (aged 6).
- cymbal crash
- vocal sobbing

c) Got a pet dog (aged 5).
- vocal 'woof'
- maracas for wagging tail
- claves for walking

d) Cried on my first day at school (aged 4).
- vocal sobbing
- other children saying playground chant
- running footsteps
- reassuring teacher's voice

e) Went to the fair (aged 3).
- chattering voices
- footsteps
- jingle bells for money
- vocal humming for roundabout
- tape of pop song for ride

Extension Activity

The children might like to find appropriate actions to go with their sounds.

Music Attainment Target: 1
Main Focus: Exploring and Composing
Key Stage: 1

History Attainment Target: 1
Main Focus: Chronological Order

Greek Mythology

Suggested Materials

See chart opposite.

Suggested Listening:

The Planets Suite by Holst.

1. Divide the children into groups. Give each group a description of one of the Greek (or Roman) gods on the chart.
2. After discussing the description, ask the groups to compose a short piece to match it.
3. Encourage the children to think of two types of sound to help plan their music:

    a) background sounds
    b) sound effects.

The suggestions on the chart may help.

Extension Activities

Children may recognize that some of the Roman gods (in brackets) have planets named after them. They may like to listen to some extracts from *The Planets Suite* by Holst. Some extracts (like 'Mars') are often used for TV programmes, and so the children may recognize them. They could discuss whether the 'Mars' music sounds war-like, and if so, why.

Music Attainment Target: 1
Main Focus: Composing
Key Stage: 2

Core Study Unit: 5
Main Focus: Ancient Greece

GODS	BACKGROUND	SOUND EFFECTS
Poseidon (Neptune) - god of the sea. He could cause wild furious storms, and yet could send good winds to calm them down again.	Ebbing and flowing. (Glockenspiels glissando up and down.)	Lightning, huge waves, rain and winds. (Cymbals, vocal wind sounds, patting knees, chime bar pattern, clapping.)
Ares (Mars) - god of war. Hated by all the other gods. God of blind, brutal destruction. Went to war accompanied by his two sons, Fear and Fright.	Threatening, warning 'throb'. (Drumbeat repeated throughout. Low vocal humming sounds.)	Fighting - destruction. (Vocal cries, cymbals, claves, drum.)
Hades (Pluto) - ruled the Underworld, a place of limbo, where the dead wandered around like pale shadows.	Spooky. (High vocal screeching sounds. Meandering humming sounds.)	Ghosts. (Vocal 'Oooohs'. Claves for footsteps. Violin bow or brushes drawn across edge of a cymbal.)
Apollo (Apollo) - god of light, music and archery. Also sudden death.	Brightness. (Random notes on glockenspiels. Softly beaten cymbal.)	Arrows, sudden noises. (Loud beat on drum. Cymbal crash. Vocal 'Shhuh' for arrows.)
Aphrodite (Venus) - goddess of love and gardens.	Beautiful, peaceful sounds. (Random notes on pentatonic chimes, gently shaken maracas for soft breezes.)	Flowers growing, birds singing. (Indian bells, vocal bird sounds, gentle glissandos on xylophones.)

The Olympics

Suggested Materials

A variety of percussion. Sheets of paper and something to draw with.

The present Olympic Games are based on those originally held in Ancient Greece, which were a religious festival in honour of Zeus. The original games had chariot races, boxing and wrestling, running, discus, javelin, and the pentathlon (jumping, running, javelin, discus, and wrestling).

Below is an idea for a composition based on the games.

1. Ask each member of a group of children to find two notes to be played repetitively on a xylophone, glockenspiel, or chime bar, to represent the runners' footsteps. They should practise together, each playing their two notes in unison. Can they find a way of representing this pattern visually? For example:

2. Can another group find sounds for the long jump (e.g. a tapping sound getting faster, then a pause followed by a crash on a cymbal or tambourine)? Again, can the group find a symbol for these sounds? For example:

3. The sound for the discus might be represented by the sound of finger tips scraped in a circular motion on the skin of a drum or tambour. What symbol might be used for this sound?

For example:

4. If you have a swannee whistle this could provide the sound of the javelin rising and then falling through the air. Alternatively, notes ascending then descending on a xylophone could be used. A symbol for this sound might be:

5. Once the children have decided on all the sounds, these could be recorded on a score such as the one below, with children playing their sounds in the appropriate place. It may help to point from left to right to indicate the place in the score.

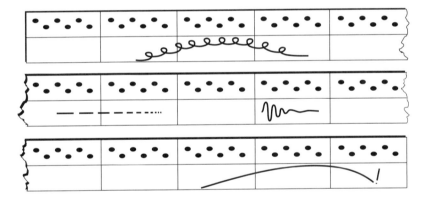

Music Attainment Target: 1
Main Focus: Composing and Recording
Key Stage: 2

Core Study Unit 5
Main Focus: Ancient Greece

Ancient Egypt

Suggested Materials

Xylophones, glockenspiels, chime bars. You will need combinations of the following bars: C, D, E♭, F♯, G.

Children work in pairs.

1. Using the notes C and G one child plays a drone.
2. The second child uses the notes C, D, E♭, F♯, and G to improvise a melody. S/he finds a short tune and practises with the drone accompaniment, until it can be performed with confidence.
3. The children choose a symbol such as a hieroglyphic or a pyramid to represent their tune, e.g.

4. The children then make up a second tune, about the same length as the first, and choose a different symbol, e.g.

5. They now order their symbols into a short sequence, e.g.

   or

   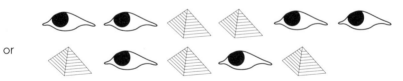

6. Once they can play their piece with confidence, they could perform it to others. The children may like to experiment with other combinations of notes.

Music Attainment Target: 1 and 2
Main Focus: Composing and Form
Key Stage: 2

Supplementary Study Unit C
Main Focus: Ancient Egypt

Roman Britain

Suggested Materials

Access to a variety of percussion, vocal and environmental sounds.

Suggested Listening

'Sounds of the Roman World' produced and published by 'Archaeologia Musica', PO Box 92, Cambridge CB4 1PU.

If you are doing a project on Roman Britain you could use the sound trail below, along with some of the suggested sounds in brackets. (This idea could be adapted for use in projects on the Vikings, the Normans, Explorers, etc.)

    a. Peaceful village. (Vocal sounds - birds singing, bees buzzing.)
    b. A shout goes out, 'The Romans!'. (Marching sounds.)
    c. The Romans attack. (Metallic sounds, e.g. kitchen utensils. Shouting on both sides.)
    d. The Romans lay new roads. (Tapping sounds, e.g. claves and woodblocks.)
    e. Bathing in the Roman baths. (Glissandos on glockenspiels, swirling maracas.)
    f. Haggling in the Roman market place. (Vocal crowd sounds, arguments, etc.)

Music Attainment Target: 1 Main Focus: Composing Key Stage: 2	Core Study Unit: 1 Main Focus: Roman Britain

Tudor and Stuart Composers

Suggested Materials

Sheets for the children to fill in as below:

Suggested Listening

Recording of 'Dido's Lament' from the opera *Dido and Aeneas* by Purcell. (For further listening suggestions see below.)

1. Play 'Dido's Lament' to the children. While they listen to the music, ask them to write down what the music makes them think about, or feel, putting one or two words in each bubble.

2. Discuss with the children what they have written, and why. What was it about the music that produced their responses? (Remember, there are no 'right' or 'wrong' answers.)

3. This activity can be repeated with different extracts of music, for example:

   From the Tudor period, extracts of madrigals, sacred music, or lute music, by composers such as Weelkes, Morley, Wilbye, Gibbons, Byrd, and Dowland. Such music often appears on compilations.

   From the Stuart period, music to choose from could include: *Canon* for Strings and Continuo by Pachelbel; the beginning of *Gloria* by Vivaldi; Suite no.3 in D by J.S. Bach; Hornpipe from the *Water Music* by Handel.

Music Attainment Target: 2 Main Focus: Appraising Key Stage: 2	Core Study Unit: 2 Main Focus: Tudors and Stuarts

The Gunpowder Plot

Suggested Materials

Access to a variety of tuned and untuned percussion. Body and vocal sounds.

1. The plotters gather together to make a secret plan. (Vocal whispering sounds; quiet drone on tuned percussion - try to find two notes that give a feeling of suspense when played together; tick-tock of a clock.)

2. Guy Fawkes guards the gunpowder, but is discovered. (Sequence of four notes repeated - try to find four notes that give a feeling of suspense; footstep sounds, quiet at first, then getting louder; vocal shouts as Guy Fawkes is discovered, plus instruments rattled and shaken.)

3. The other plotters flee for their lives. (Coconut shells for horses galloping away, getting quieter as they disappear into the distance; tulip blocks and woodblocks could also be used. Repeat sequence as the soldiers give chase.)

4. Fight between plotters and soldiers. (Thunderclaps, or claves and woodblocks tapped for gunfire.)

There are various ways of ending this trail: perhaps a slow drumbeat dying away, or the children could recite the rhyme 'Remember remember the 5th of November', or alternatively it could end with a trail representing a firework display.

(See activity '**Fireworks**' in *Poetry and Rhyme* for an example.)

Extension Activities

Some of the children could mime the story of the plot to the accompaniment of the sounds they have created.

Music Attainment Target: 1 Main Focus: Composing Key Stage: 2	Core Study Unit: 2 Main Focus: Stuarts

Civil War

Suggested Materials
Metallic objects (e.g. pots, pans, cheese graters), classroom percussion, junk, vocal and body percussion. Tape-recorder.

Suggested Listening
'Galliard Battaglia' (1621) by Samuel Scheidt (CDE 84096 or cassette KE 77096). A useful recording which includes music of the Tudor and Stuart periods is *Instruments of the Middle Ages and Renaissance*, a book and two records by the Early Music Consort of London with David Munrow (HMV SLS 988).

1. Discuss with the children the sounds that would be heard during a battle, e.g. clashing of swords, rattle of armour; horses trotting, galloping, whinnying; fanfares, shouting, the giving of orders, cries.
2. Talk about the use of appropriate sound makers to match these sounds. Divide the class into groups and make them responsible for organizing the sound of one aspect of the battle, for example:

    Group 1 - Horses
    Group 2 - Armaments and fighting sounds
    Group 3 - Sounds of the soldiers

    The groups may then wish to subdivide to make small groups responsible for specific aspects, for example:

    Group 1 - Horses: a) galloping/trotting, etc., b) whinnying/snorting
    Group 2 - Armaments: a) sounds of armour in hand-to-hand combat, b) sounds of swords clashing, c) guns and cannons
    Group 3 - Soldiers: a) shouting orders, b) cries, c) footsteps, running/walking, etc.

3. When groups have decided how they are going to represent their sounds, they can build up a sound picture together. The teacher should give very clear starting and stopping signals, e.g. pointing to group to play, raising palm of hand when a group is to stop playing.

4. When this is established, allow the children the opportunity to conduct. What do the children notice about the performance? Are there any points they wish to refine, such as a more gradual build up of sound? Perhaps the sounds of clashing swords may have been overbearing and therefore the balance of sound should be discussed. If possible make a tape of the performance, as this can aid discussion.

Extension Activities

The following music from more recent times may also evoke the idea of war. Discuss with the children how each composer achieved the effect he wanted.

Extract from *Richard III* by William Walton; the opening of the 1st movement of Symphony No. 6 by Mahler; the opening of the 1st movement of Symphony No. 5 by Shostakovich; the final section of the *1812 Overture* by Tchaikovsky.

History Attainment Target: 1 Main Focus: Composing Key Stage: 2	Core Study Unit: 2 Main Focus: Tudors and Stuarts

The Plague

Suggested Materials

Access to a variety of instruments.
Copies of cards A and B (see below).

1. Divide the class into several groups. Give each group either card A or B. It is useful if, at this point, the children do not know the viewpoints expressed on other groups' cards.

   Viewpoint A – You are a prosperous family who live in London at the time of the plague. Luckily you have managed to escape from the doomed city and have eventually made your way to a small village deep in the heart of the countryside. You happily look forward to a fresh new start in this village.

   Viewpoint B – You live in a small village in the heart of the English countryside. You and your fellow villagers hear that a family from London have come to live in your village. You know that London is stricken with the plague. What else might they have brought with them from London other than their goods and chattels? Do they pose a threat to life in your sleepy little village?

2. Ask the children to think carefully about the moods and feelings involved in viewpoint A or B. They may wish to brainstorm some words in their groups to reflect these, e.g.

   Viewpoint A - happy, lucky, hopeful, joyous, merry, lively.

   Viewpoint B - scared, worried, depressed, frightened, pessimistic, threatened, sad.

3. Ask the children to compose some 'mood' music to reflect their viewpoints. What sounds/patterns would best reflect the feelings, played in what way? For example:

Viewpoint A - fast drum pulse, 'skipping' tune on glockenspiels, tambourines tapped and bells shaken. Vocal cheers 'Hip hip hooray'.

Viewpoint B - Very slow repetitive throb on drum, slow repeated sequence of low notes on bass xylophone, vocal whispering, 'shimmering' cymbals.

Extension Activities

Divide the children into groups, and allocate one of the sounds from the above activity to each group, e.g. bells shaken, or shimmering cymbals.

Can the children find appropriate symbols to go with their sound?

e.g. Skipping tune on glockenspiel

Tambourines tapped

Once a group has decided on a symbol, discuss with the rest of the class if they feel that the chosen symbol represents the sound. Later the symbols could be grouped to produce a record of the children's compositions.

Music Attainment Target: 1
Main Focus: Composing
Key Stage: 2

Core Study Unit: 2
Main Focus: Stuarts/Viewpoints

The Great Fire of London

Suggested Materials

Access to a variety of percussion. Paper.

The Fire of London gives us excellent material for a story trail.

1. The fire starts in a bakery in Pudding Lane. (Suggestions: Scrunching paper, claves and castanets getting louder, twigs breaking - these sounds to be maintained throughout.)

2. The fire quickly spreads from one house to another. (As in 1, plus vocal wind sounds, rubbing skins of drums and/or tambours.)

3. Explosives are used to try to halt the progress of the fire. (As in 1, plus loud drum(s) and cymbal for explosion, sounds of debris falling to earth.)

4. Boats loaded with people escaping across the Thames. (Splashing water sounds, vocal cries, hands rubbing various objects for water lapping. Sounds from 1 become quieter.)

5. Progress of fire is halted. (Sounds from 1 die away leaving stillness. Everyone absolutely quiet. Maybe a solemn drum beat.)

The children could work in groups to portray one of the parts of the story. This music could be put together as background to a narrative of the story.

Music Attainment Target: 1 Main Focus: Composing Key Stage: 2	Core Study Unit: 2 Main Focus: Stuarts

Victorian Children

Suggested Materials

Access to a variety of percussion. Copies of cards A and B (see below).

> **A** You are a working child who has to get up very early to go to work in a mill. You have a long walk to work, and work a long hard day with little to eat or drink. Your job is to keep the mill floor clean, and this sometimes involves crawling under machines which can be very dangerous. After your day's work you walk back home, eat a paltry meal, and curl up on your mattress exhausted.
>
> **Ingredients for your music**
>
> A low, sorrowful sequence of notes on a xylophone, repeated.
> Repeated rhythm to represent the machines at the mill.
> Vocal sighs. 2 cockerel calls.
> Slow repeated drumbeat for slow, tired footsteps.

> **B** You are a rich child who lives a very privileged life. You live in a big house with lots of servants. You are taught each day by a governess but you also have lots of time to play with your many toys. When you go out you travel in a carriage drawn by horses.
>
> **Ingredients for your music**
>
> A fast 'skipping' tune played on a glockenspiel - repeat as you wish.
> 6 bell sounds to represent calling servants. 4 giggles.
> Repeated sound of horses' hoofs.
> 'Tick tock' sounds played on claves, to represent your many clockwork toys.

1. Divide the class into several groups. Give each group card A or card B.

2. Ask the children to read the card carefully, and using their own ideas and the suggestions on the card, mix their 'ingredients', producing a piece of music to perform to the rest of the class.

Music Attainment Target: 1	Core Study Unit: 3
Main Focus: Composing	Main Focus: Victorians / Viewpoints
Key Stage: 2	

Victorian Market

Suggested Materials
A variety of tuned percussion.

Suggested Listening
'Who will Buy?', from the musical *Oliver* by Lionel Bart (for listening to after completion of this activity).

Lavender Lady	'Sweet lavender, sweet lavender,
	Who'll buy sweet lavender?'
Broom Seller	'New brooms, maids, new brooms,
	Buy my new brooms
	To sweep your rooms.
	New brooms, maids, new brooms.'
Tinker	'Have you any work for a tinker, mistress?
	Old brass, old pots, or kettles,
	I'll mend them all with a tink terry tink,
	And never hurt your metals.'
Pear Seller	'Pears for pies,
	Come feast your eyes,
	Come feast your eyes.
	Ripest pears
	Of every size –
	Who'll buy?
	Who'll buy?'
Apple Seller	'Here are fine golden pippins –
	Who'll buy them, who'll buy?
	No one in London sells better than I,
	Who'll buy them, who'll buy?'

1. Children in groups are given a market cry to work on. Ask the children to make up a tune for the cry so that they can sing to sell their wares.

Tips to help:
- Remind the children to use the rhythms of the words for their tune. It might help them to chant and clap their cry through several times before proceeding.
- Some of the cries have repeated lines. The children might find it useful to use the same tune for both lines.

2. Having decided on the tune, groups can work on singing them fluently.

Extension Activities

Build up a class piece based on a Victorian street-market scene.

What order should the cries go in?
Should they overlap?
Should they be as loud as each other?

Research task: Street pianos (sometimes mistakenly called 'barrel organs') were often used at this time. The children might find out what they looked like, how they worked, and what they were used for. The pianoforte (piano) became very popular at this time. What does the name mean, and why was the instrument so named?

Music Attainment Target: 1 & 2
Main Focus: Appraising and Melody
Key Stage: 2

Core Study Unit: 3
Main Focus: Victorians

Modern Influences

Suggested Materials

A map of the world.

Suggested Listening

Music of Bob Marley, music by UB40, 'I shot the Sherrif' by Eric Clapton, any reggae music by other musicians.

Bhangra music. (Available from record libraries and record shops. Look for music on the 'Multitone', 'Oriental', and 'Saint' labels.)

During the years after the Second World War, people of other countries were encouraged to come to Britain. The music of these countries has influenced our listening, and two of the strongest influences have been reggae, which originated in the West Indies, and more recently bhangra beat, with its roots in the music of India.

Popular music in Britain has also been influenced by music from other countries (most notably the U.S.A.), particularly through jazz and rock and roll, which, like reggae, have their roots in the music of Africa.

1. Listen to a piece of reggae music. What do the children notice about the music? Is it music to sit and listen to, or does it make them want to dance? Can they identify any of the instruments being played (e.g. bass guitar, drums, trumpets, guitars, saxophones, percussion, keyboards, vocals)? Do they notice any parts of the music that are continually repeated?

2. Repeat this activity with some bhangra pop music. Are any of the instruments used similar to those heard in the previous piece? Do they recognize any others (e.g. different types of drums - dholak, tabla, dhol), plucked string instruments (e.g. tumbi), synthesizers, vocals. What is the mood of the music? Do they notice any difference in the singing? Are any parts of the music repeated?

(Do not feel that you or the children have to name all the instruments in a piece of music. Broad classifications such as 'drums' or 'low sounds' are perfectly acceptable, and encourage the children to listen to and talk about the music.)

3. The children might like to say which of the two extracts they prefer, and why.

Extension Activities

Discuss with the children which instruments used in modern music have been around for a long time (e.g. orchestral instruments, piano, drums, tabla, guitar), and which are adapted from older instruments (e.g. electric guitar, keyboard, synthesizers, drum machines).

Which of these instruments tend to be used within different forms? (e.g. jazz - brass, drums; reggae - guitars, drums; bhangra - synthesizers, tabla; rock music - electric guitars, drums; rap - synthesizers, etc.)

| Music Attainment Target: 2
Main Focus: Listening
Key Stage: 2 | Core Study Unit: 4
Main Focus: Britain since 1930 |

Timeline

Suggested Materials

Two short extracts of music composed in different periods in history.

Suggested Listening

Extracts from two contrasting pieces e.g.

    a) A waltz by J. Strauss (1825-1899) and an extract of disco music.
    b) A short extract from music by Mozart (1756 - 1791) and Arnold Schoenberg (1874-1951).
    c) A folk song and a pop song, played by the school recorder group.
    d) A traditional hymn and a modern hymn.

1. Play the two extracts to the children. (Ask them to close their eyes as this will focus their listening.)
2. Having put the children into groups, play the two extracts again and this time ask the children to think about which was composed first.
3. After discussion time ask the groups to report back to the whole class, giving the order in which they thought the extracts were composed, and the reasons for their decision.
4. Reveal the true order and identity of the pieces. It may be useful to represent the composers' dates on a timeline e.g.

5. Compare and contrast the two extracts with the whole class, considering the differences between the pieces, the similarities, the instruments used, which extract they preferred, and why.

Attainment Target: 2	Attainment Target: 1
Main Focus: Listening	Main Focus: Changes over a period of time
Key Stage: 2	

Appendix

Glossary

Crescendo	Getting louder.
Decrescendo	Getting quieter.
Drone	One or more notes maintained throughout a piece.
Dynamics	The gradations of volume in music.
Form	The order in which different ideas appear in a piece of music.
Improvisation	Composing spontaneously while performing.
Glissando	The process of moving from one note to another quickly, while playing all other notes in between.
Notation	The symbolic written representation of sound(s).
Ostinato	A rhythm or melody pattern repeated regularly during a piece of music (often as accompaniment).
Pitch	The perception of sounds as 'high' or 'low' in relation to each other. A woman's voice is usually higher in pitch than a man's.
Pulse	A repetitive, regular beat (sometimes silent), which can indicate the speed of a piece of music.
Rest	'Musical silence' – the absence of a sounding note or notes.
Rhythm	The pattern which long and short sounds and rests make when heard in sequence.
Rhythmic independence	The ability to maintain a rhythm against other rhythms.
Score	A written record of all the parts in a piece of music.
Sequencing	The ordering of sounds.
Timbre	The characteristics/colour of sound(s).
Volume	The loudness or quietness of sound/music.

Symbols

f	Loud
p	Quiet
$<$	Getting louder
$>$	Getting quieter

Pentatonic Scales

The notes on tuned percussion should be arranged with long bars to the left, getting increasingly smaller to the right-hand side, and in alphabetical order. Most (but not all) start with 'C'.

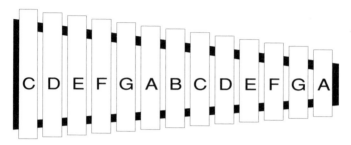

By removing any note 'B' and any note 'F', it is possible to have a five-note scale, called 'Pentatonic' (Penta = five). This should leave a sequence of C D E G A.

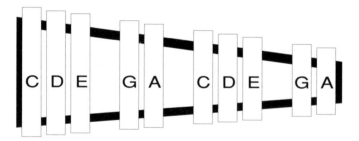

A pentatonic scale is useful for improvising melodies, both solo and in group work.

Occasionally instruments will come with notes called 'sharps' (with a ♯ after the letter), and 'flats' (with a ♭ after the letter), e.g. C♯ E♭ F♯ G♯ B♭. By using only these notes, it is again possible to create a pentatonic scale. This same scale can be found by just using the black notes on a piano or keyboard. Use this scale if most of the notes on your tuned percussion are sharps and flats.